Praise for *Newspaper Reading*

"JC Crumpton's writing seems simplistic, yet its complexity reveals itself in layers of meaning. His ability to transcend makes this collection both universally appealing and emotively valuable. His words become the dance and we the dancers find rhythm and cadence in each poem. Despite the tragic echoes of despair, hope is the steadfast thread that I am left holding in the end...I felt like I knew these speakers and characters because I do. They are me and they are those I know at some point before or now."

—Shannon Rucci Vance, ENG121 and LIT115 teacher,

Denver, Colorado

"This selection of poetry will take you on an enthralling journey of nostalgia, contemplation, and reflection, that will in turn evoke feelings and emotions that will compel you to want to dive deeper...JC has the unique ability to create a myriad of layers within his writing – I have read many of these over and over, finding new and hidden treasures each time. Not to be missed!"

—Louise Thomas, NHS, Newcastle upon Tyne, United Kingdom

"Loss, Anger, Memory, Journeys are the categories of this collection of poems. It's like four boxes placed before you. It is not surprising if your hand trembles as you choose. JC goes to those places, the places you might prefer to avoid, the bare bones real stuff, ashes, and darkness; however, he never takes us to resolutions we expect. Holding our breath we follow and find tenderness enough to keep reading."

—Crow Johnson Evans, songwriter, musician, author, artist,

Northwest Arkansas

Newspaper Reading

poetry collection

JC Crumpton

Carter Vaye Productions, LLC

Newspaper Reading

Poetry collection

JC CRUMPTON

for my teachers and mentors, both formal and those that never knew who they were but who taught me nonetheless.

Contents

LOSS

Time to Save the World

I went to leave but other cars had blocked me
so I went back in since I was already
where I wanted to be. We danced and we danced
and we danced. Back then we had time to hang
with friends and still had plenty to discuss
how the world needed saving and we'd be the ones
to do it—right after college and careers and kids
and retirement. Back then we always had enough.

Out on the North Way

The stars no longer sing out on the North Way,
the foundations once set are cracked and crumbling—
truth is faintly whispered like something to be feared.
The road draws long and weary after the rain
has settled the dust heavy to the ground.

Your basket of rose petals lies where it fell
—spilled—one pink and one yellow flapping in the breeze.
We watch the edges of the other's eyes,
not speaking because we know the time has come too soon.

Once we came to this same meadow with a blanket
and some food and wine. You wore a white dress.
And I brown corduroy pants and a wool vest.
The flat bread was moist and the strawberries
plump, juice running from the corner of your lips
until we kissed. Sharp cheddar and a younger
vintage of red—we could not afford then
what we have now. A breeze raised bumps
on the backs of your arms and my chest

ached tight with nervousness.

Daisies and pink poppies once grew along the stone

fence row. Winter is not the time to come here,

dirtying what once was good with something that tastes

like ashes in the back of my throat

and my eyes sting when my voice catches, failing.

The Last Parade

They forgot to open the intersection for Armageddon
and the vehicles all backed up down the road
all the way to the museum and the piece of modern art
sitting in the roundabout where I once drove
around and around and around in endless circles
as a representation or protest of unguided indecision.
I bought a birthday card at the Dollar General store
on the corner where you nearly hit the Jack Russell terrier
out wandering, looking for someone to take it home.
And I mailed it to myself to pretend the world still ran
on a normal schedule, something I could use to pencil
in the things I wanted to see and do and accomplish.

I notice the little tear in the skin between the third
and fourth finger on my right hand never has fully healed
on the drive home, and I pick at it, digging and digging
at it as if I cannot wait to bleed, or feel anguish.
I am rushing home that we might be able to make it
before the whole thing starts, but this drop on the window
must have come from somewhere—did I forget the time

you said dinner would be ready—but I have an umbrella

in the trunk in case it storms during our walk there.

The Way of Dying

Reflection stares back at me
    from silver ice; and it is empty.
    The crows call one to another
    tear—only one—tumbles to the ground,
    leaves tremble beneath the breeze.

Bare feet scratch through the pebbles
    where memories once walked
    but only a void chose to remain
    to sup at a broken table and drink
    tea from a broken cup.

One calloused hand grasping a dried rose
    one open hand holding the edge of nothing
    —blood—from the tiny fingerprick
    feeds the hungry ground where it fell,
    but salted earth stays empty.

Wind singing gone silent, the dirt is scorched
and the nightingale has lost her voice.

Cobblestones

We waited at the outside table for the summer rains to come
and you mentioned no one builds with cobblestone anymore
and I noticed that the patterns in one of the stones looked like
the whirls in your coffee after you put the cream in but before
you stirred it with your spoon. That building on the corner
used to be a hotel or something but now it has an identity crisis,
marching through time with an indecisiveness like schizophrenia
as it searches for what it wants to be: a bed-and-breakfast
or an ice cream parlor or an art gallery or a leather goods boutique.

We came here once—long ago, far enough removed from now
that we were different people with different dreams and different
  hopes—
and I recalled you didn't really like the place because it smelled
like a memory you could not remember. I reached over and set my
  hand
on the table so the side of my little finger gently touched your
  thumb,
but you gasped and pulled your hand away to wave at some friends
walking down the cobblestones to meet us for a quick lunch.

Glories and Awards and Parades

You told me once you sometimes thought you wouldn't care
if you made it home. We sat in the den your mother called a lounge
with its high-back plush chairs made of camel-colored leather
and in which we felt like we were being swallowed up by monsters
when we played in them as children and before the adults came
chasing us out, clapping their hands together and scolding us
like they were shooing a stray cat from the fence.
We thought they were cross with us, but I sneaked back once
and peered quietly around the corner to see your mother
with this wistful smile she doesn't bear today.

Photos and paintings of uniformed men in serious poses
look down from the walls, and I wonder what they think
today and would we give up all our glories and awards and parades
if we could see your mother smile once again.
When I walked down the hall, the footsteps didn't sound
the same as they had all those years before and when I
left I knew there would be no reason for me to ever come back.

Ashes and Soot

I waited and wanted and watched
only to have the embers wane cold
and gray to ashes and soot, lifeless
because the fire inside will not be lit,
will not burn and will not heat
the passion and drive and desire
to do anything more than day to day.

The grasses are soft where I laid
down beside the brook and listened
to the music of movement, of wind
rustling the leaves above, rushing
the air like a long, lonely moan.
I lingered and languished to hear
a voice that remained silent and lost.

The Scar

A thin white line runs up the back of my hand
slipping between the second and third knuckles
before dropping off the edge when I curl my fingers
into a tight fist. I never remember where I earned it,
and the story changes every time I tell it
until one iteration has no resembling feature
to the last time when I told it at an office party,
where all the empty people talked politely and smiled
when they offered me something sweet from the tray
as it passed by between snippets of tepid conversation
and hurried nods of cultured refinement that said
I care enough to almost pay attention. The band
started playing and singing and swaying a melody
that really had nothing to do with the story I told,
but it was distracting enough no one even cared
that I could not remember the origins of the scar.

Maybe it came from the glass that shattered against the wall
next to my head when you told me in your most loving voice
that you didn't want me to leave, but I did anyway
and still cannot remember its beginning.

My Little Whore

It is the oldest profession and she is so very professional
in her day-to-day running of a past-time that becomes business
as usual, directed by the criminally sane only because their insanity
has become the status quo of a society doomed to destroy itself
in a storm of progress mired in the fast lane of mediocrity.
There is no way to bring her all the moon and stars
tied up in a bouquet with rainbow ribbons and gold
because the world spins so haphazardly on its axis.
Yet she demands it the way the precious diamond needs the light
to realize the depths and shallows of its beauty.

I.

The images we have lived here are scars not monuments
and unlike the words written carefully on the page
they are not memorialized and only forgotten;
they are not the foundations of empires
they do not set nation against nation,
man against man, even army against army.
All that glitters may not always be gold
but it is for her that we always quest,

covering our conquests in the noblest notions
of a humanity devoid of all but depravity.

We walk through this circuitous circumstance
of life and reluctantly search for an immortality
asleep, only dreaming and hoping for ignorance
so that we can walk through the day unaware,
hoping life means nothing more than the perfect images
of a cardboard wheel of a View-Master slide
—let's flip that green handle just to change the pictures we don't
  like.

II.

There stands a figure left alone out in the rain
waiting at that point where the day edges to the night
searching for something simple like a premonition
of what will come, what will have been written.

He wonders if her touch her kiss all her sweet caresses
will cause them to forget all the lies and moments of bliss
shattered by the staccato rhythms of chaos mixed with hesitations.

She disguises her truth with pretentious conceptions,
images that were once clear and bright
have washed out colors depicting worn lines
and the chicken in the pot turns to ash.

III.

All enter the room and ask with the lost innocence

that we once all possessed, searching for reason in the

  pandemonium

yearning for the Rockwellian painting, the picnic in the Alpine

  meadow

and warm bread fresh from the oven and melting in our mouths.

The wish cast into the well tumbles through the blue,

flashing and spinning and flipping down past the shadow line

where the blue darkens to black and it slips into never seen again.

All the wishes are soon forgotten because history

is not written by the winners—indeed, it is stone-chiseled

by fiction writers and playwrights and philosophers and those

that have the wherewithal to create the narrative as they see fit.

A homeless farmer wanders the roadside ditches, tending

his acres of dandelions and peach-colored poppies while his

  children

pass the plate at the off ramp through the rush of people going

  home.

IV.

Her beauty has slipped to that point a couple stages past faded

  elegance,

after two packs a day for two centuries has left her voice rasping

  like stone

and with canyon-like crows' feet. Her fingertips are stained yellow.

V.

If I stay, will you tell me a story without pain

If I wait, will the day after tomorrow come when bidden

The love songs keep skipping until I cannot even hear the words.

The musicians have left the studio because Local 242

has picked up the picket line, demanding hot lunches

and cinnamon-flavored coffees during the hourly breaks.

Only the street performers stayed, juggling silver hoops,

painting the same fucking caricature over and over again,

and conning a shell game with a misdirecting cast of the hand.

VI.

He waits for the lady of the lake to bring him Excalibur

that he may fight the dragon, he may fend off the barbarian hordes,

but her meth addiction has left her a wrinkled husk, limping

behind a walker with squeaky wheels because she couldn't

hold the can of WD-40 in her trembling hands.

Reprise/Epilogue.

I have gone to bed with her again,

hoping that there is no hole in the condom

and that her Syphilis has gone beyond contagious.

Her sanity has left her alone, stood up,

as Samson brings down the temple around us

punishing us for our well-meaning misgivings

that we cannot keep from leaking out the cracks

and crevasse in our hands.

An October Night after Midnight

A silver moon hung low that night not so long ago
and gray-white clouds drifted over and away and over,
blown by a higher wind than the one that drifted down
like the sky exhaled, stirring the knee-high grasses
covering the mark of your passing when you left.
You didn't smile. You didn't frown.
You didn't even cry when I crumbled to my knees.
Your slender hand reached to my cheek
but it never closed the gap, and I felt the heat
from your skin like a warmth in the coolness.

I am left with a lonely cricket, chirping and clicking,
calling out for a mate that never comes and never returns.
The dew came up early, scattered across the field
like tiny shards of a shattered mirror broken on the floor,
piebald reflections of that orb, tears in the rain,
crumbs and jewels strewn over the ground.
The breath of wind stirs the leaves and the grass and my hair,
and I look down to see my hands have not moved
from where they rest against the tops of my thighs.

Broken

I know the music is over when You fold your arms
like that against your chest as if the windows opened
to let winter settle over the air between Us.
We sat at either end of the old tattered couch,
You looking out the side window to the two dogs
rooting through the flower bed, chasing a rabbit
or the squirrels that scamper up the broad oak
across the roof and down into the backyard, leaping
over the yawning chasm to the post we set up for the birds,
Me watching the powerless television, the screen grayed
but showing the events that happen behind Us,
the fan blades spinning around and around and around
the little tassels swaying back and forth, side to side
and the three lights casting shadows against the wall,
only three because the fourth bulb burned out two weeks past,
and We waited to see who would change it first.

The screen door is still broken, the metal handle
nothing but a knob on the outside and a jagged piece

inside where the latch doesn't catch and it swings out
when the storms come, slamming against the side of the house.
And in the mornings with the silver sheen of moisture still
shining on the brick and stone pathway leading from the back
to the front, We can see where the faux adobe has crumbled,
piling up on the ground in little mounds of residue,
reminders that without care it all falls apart.

The sun is shining outside and the three lights still burn,
but I wander upstairs to my study where thick red curtains
have been drawn to keep out the light so everything is cast
in shadow, and I read a book on escapism by the glow
of the banker's lamp You gave Me for my birthday last year.

Only the Clock Ticks On

When the room is silent and I put my ear to the wall
I can hear their voices—little more than whispers—
in hushed conversations filled with hidden secrets
and words they hope I cannot understand or repeat.
The white walls in the day are now bone gray
and dull from the moon peeking through the gap
where the edges of the curtains do not quite meet,
and between bitter hisses and angry gasps
I hear the ticking of the clock, counting
up—or down—with hands that cast tiny shadows
against the silver face edged with bold black numbers.

A book sits atop the table beside the bed,
bound leather with a cord wrapped around and around
to keep it tightly closed and the words from escaping.
Words you wrote down for me to read
when the night crushes in and I sit alone,
messages meant to strengthen and heal and encourage
succinct words in soft curves and gentle sounds.
Your picture hides there between random pages

when you put it there to remind me,
and I hope I still recognize you each time
I open the cover and look at it.

The voices downstairs have stopped, and I wait,
alone, with nothing left to read or write.
Only the clock ticks on and on, oblivious.

Dear John

A small picture hangs upon the wall of the room
wherein I sit with slumped shoulders
and listen to the pendulum swing to and fro.
The half-finished letter I meant to write to you
still waits upon the desk beneath the window
and a late-winter rain streaks the glass.
Fire pops and crackles in the hearth across the way
but it fails to drive out the damp and cold
and my sweater isn't enough to keep me warm.
I cannot remember all the words I wanted to say,
they do not hang unspoken from my lips
and they do not wait for me at the door.

Left and Right

From my upstairs office I can see an old man
working outside nearly every day rain or shine
in the garden edging the five concrete steps
that climb from the sidewalk to the house.
A black metal table sits in the center of his porch
with black metal chairs beside—one to either side—
and sits in the chair on his left at the day's end
when he is weary—never in the right—with the sun
peering between the houses on the other side of the street
so he has to squint with his hand raised and one eye
closed against the glare as he waves with the other hand
at all the children as they race by on their scooters,
not too different from back in their day. He looks over
at the empty chair where she used to sit, his right.

Days in the Time of Corona

Cynicism is the language of love for a generation
that never learned to hope—a voice they share
amongst the shadows where they wander aimlessly,
lamenting truthful things they lost: like their youth
and the meanings of the words the poets all wrote
and which they knew would have no purpose later on.
The sky grew overcast and the wind came up,
blowing his cries back into his face like something
he could never unload, a burden he never wanted.

He held onto a promise like a candle in the darkness,
given in a moment when strength built and waxed
until he thought he would carry the world on his shoulders.
Now the cardinal calls through the open window
where the rain enters and pools upon the floor beneath the sill,
and he wonders what they say to each other
or if it's only meaningless, as the vow spilled from forgotten lips,
all those many years ago when he only wanted hope.

An Envelope Addressed to Me

I came home the other evening
—it was winter, so the fading light
lasted next to no time at all and
gray was the only color left in the world—
and the door had been left ajar

just enough the cat had escaped.
But she didn't venture far, crouching
and looking down so she could not see
how very big the whole sky was.
The rose tree stood dormant and bare

alone in the garden crusted with thin snow
on a one-day lengthened February.
You told me just that morning the whole
season made you sick. Anticipating
the changes that never changed only worsening.

You waited alone in the living room,
with an envelope addressed to me,

40

sitting on the old faded-red cloth couch
your granny left you and that you kept
because it reminded you of Spring.

The glass of water on the table was half full
sitting neatly beside the half-eaten pastry.
I wondered how you felt,
but I never did very good at that
so I only sat quietly with my hand over yours.

ANGER

Newspaper Reading

Each morning when I step out on the porch,
and my misting breath sinks and only fades
—never to rise—
I turn to Living so I can:
fun-loving people live
fun-filled lives and
skip skip jump across the water,
skiing and laughing and playing and living.

Growing fat red tomatoes with the help
of chemical-free pesticides
is yet another thing
they tell me to do to live.
But all I can grow is my own little
darkness, festering in the corners of my heart
that sprouts little
tendrils of shadow that choke
the very breath from me.

Or attend a support-group meeting

where I introduce myself to my self

in twelve simple steps

and hack and gag and cough down two packs a night

while I listen

to sad stories of success

and joyful moments of desperation.

I seek but cannot find,

I ask but never do receive

a pamphlet

from Pueblo, Colorado on how to live,

how to breath,

and to forgive myself for being born.

November 2012

Misguided angels. Searching for something to save
bring apocalypse upon apocalypse, ashes upon ashes,
bones upon bones, until the path is paved
with their beneficence but where no foot treads
and no voice can be heard in song.
Only the wind blows—a ubiquitous lullaby,
shifting through the skeletons lining the avenue,
silent sentinels and faithful watchers of the end.

Muted

The embers have gone cold
and the darkness is complete,
its weight enveloping and smothering.
All the songs have faded
and the sun only sets
the birds in the field are quiet
the patter of the rain is silent,
the melodies are broken and scattered
across the ground like the refuse
left as the flood waters recede.

My voice has grown mute
its baritone sonances hidden,
devoid of its strength
and only half-remembered
as a flip-page show of images
with pieces torn out and missing.

Fire Sale

You left that night and took everything with you
like a fire sale where all must go or it would stay forever,
and the only thing that bothered me was the smell—
it had changed to something unfamiliar. I wept a little
for comfortable odors and typical sounds. I drank some,
and I never drank alone. I called friends and family
but hung up before they answered because I did not know
who knew what or why or who sided with you or me.

Endings are beginnings—only I didn't realize it that night
and thought that everything must be falling into chaos
because this was a path upon which I never had walked,
a route I never had taken. When the tears had crusted
and dried upon my cheeks, I strode purposefully upstairs
to the master bathroom and left the toilet set up.

Blue

Snow fell in spits and spurts yesterday, not cold enough
or too cold to snow I never know, and still I saw birds
that reminded me more of spring: an eastern bluebird
swept down over the gray and crusted lawn like an old A-6
on a low-altitude bombing run, swooping low and banking
up at the end to alight on the branch of a gnarled oak,
and a bluejay fluttered in the frost as if it were water

and not the crisp-edged crystal that it truly is.
Two blue notebooks sat on the table in my office,
the lid to the half-drunk water bottle was as well
as was the one I'd yet to open—vivid and bright
to the point I wondered why it is the color of melancholy.

My window looked a good twenty feet above the yard
and when I looked out, pressing my forehead up against
the glass so I could feel the bite of the cold outside,
I noticed the wind had captured a single snowflake.
It hovered within my reach but outside my fingers and my palm
like a single note in a long sad song struck at the end,

48

and I want to smile but wondered why I didn't or if I had

at all that day and I saw the band on my watch was also blue.

Something I Could Blame

I forgot that the needle always rends and tears
but nothing changes its sweet allure
even the hallucinations are the same
every time I've opened my eyes to see something
different something new and unabused

something I could blame on my mother or on my father
or even on Freud if I could pull off another fraud.
I once opened my eyes to nothing but cold and dark and silence
rushes like a crowd swishing in a to-and-fro in my ears
but I have seen this all before and heard the promises unkept
like a late-night after-the-infomercial preacher with his number
plastered bright and vivid across the television screen.

Contrasting Night & Day

Dancing alone in the darkness
slam and grunt and pretend to mate
or love while the beat pushes down
—driving into the brain
until reason has slipped beneath
the pressure of six or sixteen shots
of fragile potency like butternipple.

The cannibals in the suits and ties
couple on the altar
taking and stealing and raping
for the sweet megalomaniac high-high
that spreads through the ether of their minds
and feeds their daily living
like devotionals at breakfast time.

Everything still tastes of bitterness
smells of mothballs and formaldehyde and arsenic
deep down amid the mixture of fire and brimstone
where some little man in red pajamas

sits the bench and judges the best
of those takers of the seven—
sweet virtuous seven deadly desires.

They fail to see the convulsions—
the trembling of world and moral experiments
that have touched the edges of propriety
and slips out through the cage
to rant and rage and scream and thrash
while the rest of humanity cries out
to false-gods that no longer hear their voices.

The message is self-genocide
taught in schools and churches and assembly lines
where we stamp out product after product
only to have stomped to death
quality and replaced it with pestilence
that reeks of forgotten promises
broken vows and indulgences.

The Dynamic of the Vacuum

Arctic nights are beautiful when the clouds are gone
where the stars shine brightly in the empty space
of space. It is the dynamic of the vacuum—
like politicians, stars that shine so brightly and full
of hope—out of reach and the distance between them
is abandoned but for the whispers of all the songs
they sing back and forth only to each other.

The Ghosts in the Laundry

The spirit-world is speaking to me in hushed
tones of innuendo and tiny flirtations with the reality of
poltergeists;
today at the *Sugar Creek Laundry* I felt as if I wasn't alone:
unbidden images came to mind, memories I wished
to leave dead and buried for all eternity if I might;
a dryer tumbling around and around and around in anger
at its load threw out its insides every few minutes,
and air occasionally brushed the back of my arms,
sending chills racing like cold fire along the edges of my nerves.

Unbidden memories and hated memories and memories
of being left to face the darkness alone and huddled in the corner
with the dark-beasts barking and growling and snapping
but never marking the skin, only leaving bruises to the soul
like a wet towel beat over your back one hundred times.
Visions of standing on the stairs watching the door close on my
flower that says it must be picked and smelled and loved by
another.
These haunts and recollections empowered and possessed the

54

clothes

in that strange machine, enabling it to jump out and shout at me:

You cannot close the door on us; you cannot heat us to oblivion;

we are here to stay, spun around and around and around

but always here as the ghosts in the laundry.

No One Heard Me Scream Today

The traffic seemed thicker today, more congealed
along the arteries and veins that directed each vessel
here and there. With the windows rolled up and the music
playing loud and harsh and bitter, no one heard me scream.

The old man walked his black lab by the intersection
this morning the same as he does most every day.
The air conditioning in my car churned out cold air
on high, but he wore a thick flannel shirt like lumberjacks
in the Pacific Northwest used to wear. If it had been raining
or ten degrees cooler, he would have worn a black beanie
like the dockworkers do back east in the cold, salty spray.
A tiny bead of sweat rolled down the bridge of my nose,
and before the light turned green, the old man knelt
to bag the dog's deposit but struggled and heaved and pulled
on his walking stick so he and his friend might continue on.

Clowns on Parade & Fluffy Things

I thought I saw something among the clouds
the other day, but it must have been only my imagination
and the big expansive sky frightens me—so bad—
that I cringe and cower and cannot go outside.

A man beneath the underpass holds a cardboard sign
with painstakingly and carefully and slowly-drawn words:
PUNISHED & ENSLAVED.

We can share grief, we can share sympathy,
we can feel empathy, we can take a shoulder offered,
but ultimately when the light fades, we suffer alone.

Anger in Fairytale Land

I'll taste your sacrifice amidst the chaos.
In anger I become what others hate:
You see upon my table there way off
It is dinner that makes the Rabbit late.
Flee with those that run with Chicken Little,
Running headless from swiftly falling skies,
And screaming like those stampeding cattle
From me, death, who takes their fairytale lives.
All the king's horses and all the king's men
Though they tell Humpty that they'll do their best,
Will not ever try to put him back again
Because he was scrambled for my breakfast.
And though Jack rolls down the hill with laughter,
Dear sweet Jill will not come tumbling after.

MEMORY

Eating Soup at a Coffee Shop

You approached in tiny little half steps, maybe slowing time
because it raced around you with such fierce velocity
your hair stirred in the breeze it left rushing along.
You ate your chicken-cheese tortilla soup with tiny sips,
maybe because it scalded your mouth after you refused the ice
chips the barista offered you and you dabbed at your mouth
with only the end of the napkin, drying the liquid clinging to the
    corners.
You finished with a flourish, scooping up the remnants
in quicker and quicker scoops, chasing the last bit of soup
that hid and fled and sought to remain free and unconsumed.
You opened your cookie like it was treasure, something to cherish
something to relish, something that you hope would last
and maybe it would if you were careful. But time kept rushing
and by the moment your phone buzzed, the cookie was gone.

Lessons Learned Skipping School

These are the boughs that are broken
the moist scents of earth and moss fill the air
and I'm reminded of youthful innocence
afternoons beneath the skies and leaves
instead of brick-and-mortar halls
where they taught us things we never wanted to learn.

Are we any better off now that we learned them anyway?
And we try to protect our progeny from experiencing innocence
and our pasts that we survived frighten us even more
because we fear it shall become their present.

It was only a kiss. The string of hair that fell across
the bridge of her nose still wet from our swim beneath the bluff,
ginger against soft cream. Supple lips and her palms
warm even though her arm pimpled
when I traced the veins and tendons on the back of her hand—
if only Scott and Laura had come back sooner
or we had been too shy to step from our present into our tomorrow.

Theo's

The wind blew cold that night,
but I don't know if that is why I shivered
or if it was because of the passionless speech
we spoke in order to bridle all the passions

that needed to be verbalized
in order for it to not fester and ooze.

They only had one table open
—we'll take it, thank you—
waiting for us in the middle,
visible to all the eyes that looked up
and glanced away so they could not see
that they'd been seen.

The steak was undercooked for my taste,
like the conversation, but flavorful
so that my mind wondered between dinner
and all those big, little things bothering you.

We heard snippets and pieces of music
and private conversations—and I understood
why we came: because to remember tomorrow,
I wanted you to enjoy today.

The Box

I even read a book on the subject,
several times, and still I failed.
I told you once that there is no box—
not in the same way there is no spoon,
but something more existential and livid and binding—
that you could tear down all the walls around you
that no fetters would ever hold you
that no idea could be constrained
that nothing need ever hold you back.

The nights are long now, the shadows deep
and impenetrable down where the monsters hide.
I saw you in a passing moment the other day
with your shoulders hunched and your eyes down,
we never spoke, and I never asked how you were.
Looking down and never up, all we see
are the cracks and crevices and dirt and grime
we miss everyday beautiful, replacing it with all the ugly.

I remember the last time we laughed together.

I remember the last time we cried together.

Now I see the end in the days waiting for us

and my eyes have blurred and my vision falters.

This shattered home crumbles beyond repair,

my hands are calloused and mangled and bloody

I've not enough fingers to stem the leaking.

Longing for those Saturday mornings when the house still slept

where we laughed and we danced with ourselves

no worries and no anger and no tears.

These fragile things have broken, slipping and falling

through gnarled hands with gnarled fingers.

I cannot be your knight I cannot bear this shield

when you embrace the monsters that whittle away

at my heart and soul piece by piece.

No darkness lasts forever, don't get lost

and left behind. Don't lose hope and don't turn back.

The shortest distance through the deepest night

is straight on through morning.

These fragile things have broken, slipping and falling

through gnarled hands with gnarled fingers.

I cannot be your knight I cannot bear this shield.

My steps become stumbles until I crawl

my eyes close and I lay my head on the cold hard ground.

A Weekend Drink

The other night while I sat at the Lightbulb
we saw a new-comer tip his glass to the reggae band, muttering:
I'll drink to those happier times you sing,
for I have known them too.

And one month later at the same club we will see
the daily-comer he had become lift his glass to the blues band,
  toasting:
I'll drink to those sadder times you cry,
because I have felt like you.

A Hanging

I watched an execution the other day
not out of some sick and morbid fascination
but just so I could tell myself it is not me
that hangs there twitching from the gallows.
I guess it's the same reason I read
all the tragedies—the more tragic and painful
and heart-wrenching and tearful the better—
to know that something horrible happens
to other people and not just to me day after day.

Saturday Night Special

Winters represent an adventure when you're young and poor
but especially ignorant to the point you don't understand
that most children our ages didn't share snow boots,
stomping about in father's shoes going clomp and clomp and
  clomp
through the crust that settled over the top of the snow
after the sun had dropped into its basement room.
But the cows Maria and Annabelle needed milked and fed
so we bundled up in a hurry to see who got the boots first.

And ramen noodles were something akin to magic
in our father's hands, how they pulled the last bit of good
out of leftovers left over through the week on Saturdays
—the last ends of Sunday's roast, always peas and carrots
or some opened and tossed in if none remained, green beans
tough and chewy, and sliced beef hot dogs if we begged hard
  enough.

Perhaps it was the long, slow simmer just below a boil
perhaps the five shakes of sodium-rich Worcestershire sauce

perhaps the mystery dry seasoning in the mysterious tin packets
gave it something special, something memorable and memorialized
like those oh so rare treats of grilled cheese sandwiches
and tomato soup while we watched animal documentaries
we had probably seen at least a hundred and one times.
We even ate the broccoli he snuck in, those nasty green stalks
that we never even fed the dog beneath the table.

Walking Among the Ruins

The garage door on the left still had a dent
sitting way down at the bottom edge behind the leaves
swept up against the chipped white aluminum with hints of rust.

I walked in the ruins of a past life,
a place that may become a future in someone else's time
and I thought I saw movement in the water that pooled
into tiny puddles among the tannish carpet beneath the holes
peering in from the ceiling. But only ripples
disturbed the surface stretching and racing and beginning.

One winter night with friends snowed from their homes,
we turned off the overheads and strung Christmas lights
from wall to wall and back again in the dining room.
We made our own dance club and moved to old Depeche Mode
and New Order and even tried to understand some Cyberaktif,
mostly we just sat and talked about dreams and things to be.

Now the window with no screen I crept in and out many times
has no glass, and something lurks down there in the basement

  shadows

at the edge of the room my father started for me

but finished for my sister. There is blood on the frame,

only I do not know if I left it today or back then.

The porch swing creaks a little as I leave, scraping

across the painted concrete and hanging only on one side

because the other slipped from its anchor long before the present.

Trust

I watch her every night as she undresses
and wonder if in all the things I have ever done
have I ever done anything to earn such trust.
Times have been hard at times and we do not live
in the grandest house, some of its contents reused,
refinished, rebuilt and turned into something else.
The garden where she should be able to sit in quiet
contemplation simply isn't—just five empty boxes,
one with a tree growing up ten feet through the neglect.
Her fingers are bare because I've yet to buy her a ring—
I proposed to her with a bright red candy ring pop
that she still has after she ate the sucker part—
but she doesn't look at it like something's missing,
at least not in those quiet moments when I watch her.

Falling from the Sky

Raining cats and dogs is something I should like to see
at least once—or maybe twice: the first time all by myself
so everyone thinks me a bit on the eccentric side—they murmur
when I pass them by in the street with their hands together
held over their mouths as they whisper and point without pointing
—and second so everyone else can see and I proudly strut
through the town square: There you go. I am not the crazy one.

Scientists have never witnessed the phenomena—so all the people
in the world over have slipped by existence without an elevator
that goes all the way to the top floor for men's clothing
and household appliances. French soldiers at Lalain were mad
when they saw toads fall from the sky just a few years
before the start of the 19th century. Did the elders laugh at the boy
in the town of Bhanvad, India when it rained fish from the sky?
Will they believe him when the moon turns to blood or will they
run him out with brooms and sticks and stones and burning brands
while the toothless old man on his porch laughs and cackles and
  wheezes?

I did see it rain ice balls once—none of my neighbors are scientists

but we saw them churning like tiny white marbles down the avenue

in the mid-afternoon torrent pouring along like a river gone mad,

they rolled across the roofs and into all the freshly-painted gutters

to make an incredible racket as they tumbled down the spouts,

piling up in little piles on the ground beside every home along the
  street.

Roger came out with a glass of bourbon poured three thick fingers
  deep

and gently plopped four of the ice balls from the stack into his
  tumbler,

but he may actually be eccentric because we only see him at
  parties.

Clock

This old photo album always creaks when you open it
and the smell of musty old memories makes you think you
  shouldn't like it
but it somehow sits soft and warm and comfortable
like those times you sat on the couch nestled between grandma on
  one side
grandpa on the other, listening to tales of times long gone
yet still remembered. How Aunt Rhonda had thrown water at your
  father
because he had spilled punch on her brand new Sunday dress.
How Uncle Shorty always dressed up as that fat old man in red
each and every Christmas much to the delight of the kids
even when they grew old enough to know better,
even when they grew wise enough to recognize the coffee on his
  breath.

Ronnie Milsap is playing on Pappy's old radio beneath the
  window,
a crooning tune about not wanting to know, about hiding
from learning how the story ends and nothing comes after,

only heartache and heartbreaks and pain and loss.

It took me years to understand, to realize why we looked

through these old albums when so many of them are gone now.

They are captured here, moments in time with beginnings

and the endings aren't revealed in the pictures

because there are smiles and laughter and love

like this time when you watched the children open presents,

sitting on that decrepit, sunken-cushioned sofa in your blue robe,

hair disheveled like you'd just awakened when you hadn't even
  slept

gray slippers with the hole on the side where the sole had separated

from the body—you can't even see that I gave you new, softer ones

only minutes later and we threw the old ones away in the
  evening—

sitting on the orange carpet that was all the rage back then.

Some of the pictures have slid out of place on the next page

coming off the adhesive back, wedging down behind another
  snapshot

of a captured moment that had somehow slipped my mind

and remained hidden in the shadows until this reminiscing.

I don't remember if it had been six or seven years

but the old clock on the wall says 1776 on one side

and 1976 on the other. It was a quiet moment

after dinner and the children had been set down for the night,

the lights were low and I had one shot left on the roll.

The plastic film over the page is brittle and starts to tear when I pull up the corner and try to set the picture straight.

My hands are trembling—too much coffee like Uncle Shorty
or is it something else creeping in—and can't quite grip it.
Does it need to be straightened, or should it remain where it is?
There but half askew, half hidden and half revealed.
I glance at the clock—the same one—but don't see the time,
instead I see that the hand moves on and on, and I cannot stop it,
and I cannot change it or alter what it does.
Today I thought that I have reached that point in life,
that point I ran from and ignored so it would not grab hold of me,
that place in time when I realize that I have started to lose more
  friends
each day than new ones entering my life to be captured in a photo.

I know why we look at these albums now and why we remember.
Ronnie had it right, and the pictures are moments
where we don't have to know how the story ends.

Shattered

I asked you to dance that night
but you said no and my ego
felt as shattered as the glass
of vodka collins I dropped earlier
in the night. Scattered ice
among the shards and clear liquid
reflecting the lights in broken
colors as chaotic as the music
I couldn't quite latch onto
through the muffled fuzz
that had descended over me
because I didn't drop any
of those first six glasses.

I Lost a Year

I lost a year somewhere in the dark last night
and you still slept beside me, breathing in and out
at almost a snore, and I wondered if you were chasing
it while you dreamt. Did it prove to be a furtive prey
that could not be cornered? Did it leap about always
slipping just beyond your grasp as your fingers closed?

In the scheme of things, I may want that year back some day.
It could be something that I need, it could be something
that I will want and cannot see myself doing without
because time is never resting where we want it to. It flees
from us, running out in those places where visions dance
and we see far less than when we were young and innocent,
when we laughed and skipped and played,
when we were grand and fancied ourselves in fairytales.

The year came back to me by the time the mirror steamed over,
and I wondered if it only left me because my aged brain
cannot seem to hold on to the things it once could, would,
if it needed to run and play and remind me that I could.

An Age of Wonder Lost

After the summer rain the little rivulets made new roads,
paths wandering in and out among the pebbles and the sticks
where some came to rest, riding the torrent or holding fast
where they remained. Erosion and decay broke apart the hard clay
and down there in the cracks, hidden in the shadows
sprouted something the crispest green I had ever seen.
I sat there watching, hoping it pushed the ground open
like a time-lapse video from a nature documentary.

Today I have forgotten the important things, giving way
to talking and showering and eating and driving and working
from one day into the next and into the years coming after.
One afternoon standing atop the Pyramid of the Moon I saw
  power—
I took the time to watch the sky darken to gray to black,
to stand before the roar of water racing down the avenue
and swirling around and around in a giant whirlpool
that filled the plaza. I knew I heard the voices of ancient sailors
crying out to the earth and sky and wind to be saved.

Yesterday when the rains came I ran with my head down,
beneath the umbrella, watching where I placed each step
so I would not ruin my shoes for the meeting I had planned.
Where did all the wonder at daily things looked on with new eyes
and shouting at the storm go? I cannot see the important things.

Accumulated Stench

Each day I pass by the alley and hold my breath
—not to block the stench of accumulated urine
and weeks-old vomit that forces my eyes to squint,
but to hope the newspaper blankets still rise and fall
with each inhale and every wheezing exhale—
waiting to see if you've moved on, abandoning
your hard-fought space there in the darkened recesses
between the two industrial dumpsters against the bricks
where you once had to kick an old man out
because he tried to claim that spot for himself.

My breath comes easier when I see the rhythms
and I hear the whistle of your in-and-out,
separated every so often by a snort or a cough.
I smile quietly, still wanting you to maybe go see
the Sisters of Infinite Grace or counselors at the YMCA,
or maybe just to see you've picked up and moved on.

Black Coals and Gray Dust

There is dust in my hand, and I don't know
where it came from—gray dust, almost like ash
from the bottom of the round, fat-bottomed grill
that father kept in the backyard where we had holidays
and birthdays and Sunday afternoons and celebrations
where he invited his dead-beat brother Uncle David
and Aunt Wife-of-the-month whose names we forgot
the very moment they walked through the wooden gate
because he'd bring another one by for the next event.

Father insisted he'd beat the rain during one June weekend,
but the sky opened up and swamped out the afternoon party
forcing everyone but me back inside where mother fixed a lunch
of roast beef sandwiches with horseradish and mayo and lettuce
and thick slices of cheddar she picked up form the deli
down on the corner earlier in the day because she disagreed
with father about the weather, only she never told him.

I thought I was alone as I watched big fat rain drops
tumble through the sky and hiss and spit and sizzle

on the coals father took such pride and care to stoke up
into the perfect heat for the thick and juicy ribeye steaks.
The coals turned black and tumbled over, and the water
turned them first to ash and then into a thickened sludge
that fell from my splay-fingered hands in plopping chunks
that splashed and plonked through the carbon-crusted grill.

When I looked up and saw him watching the gray rain
a shiver of surprise rippled across the back of my shoulders
and I smiled over at him, but his eyes did not see me.
He sat in one of the big, wooden patio chairs with a beer
unopen in his left hand the grill tongs in his right
as his unseeing eyes looked out on the ruined celebration.

The dust in my hand is a puzzle that I cannot understand
like the enigma of what my father thought as the rain fell
and the voices and the laughter drifted through the screen behind
him where the party had wandered, and I do not know
where it goes when the wind blows it from my palm.

JOURNEYS

Mr. Finley Went to the Fair

He never expected to find the marker beneath the tree
that stood in the upper corner of the north field,
an old oak spreading thick limbs over the stone fence.
It made sense in the end, the view spread out
overlooking the valley and the modest house on a rise
above the river. He did not remember the name
written anywhere in the deeds or etched on the mantle.

Davin Beau Finley. All alone beneath a tree on a hill
in some forgotten and neglected part of Johnson County.
June 6, 1944 was a day of all days to enter the world,
and on the twelfth of November seventy years later Philea
landed on a comet—did it streak the sky that night?

He never found the name in the house, so he wondered
who told Mr. Finley's stories, who shed a tear or two,
and who laid him here in this spot so he could rest.
Was he the man who took his hat off at the table
or tipped its brim when he passed a young woman
on a Saturday afternoon at the market on the square?

Did the love of his life lay him here? The one he met
at the autumn fair but thought he would never come back
so she married another? Because she doesn't lay beside him.

Was there only a quiet service at the small country church,
or was the corner the end of a parade and procession with a band
playing When the Saints Go Marching In like he sometimes hears
they do in New Orleans? It was quiet up here in this field,
and he brushed away the twig that had fallen on the stone.

A Long Release

You burden yourself with my problems
a weight that cripples you into that hunched
over way of walking. The tonnage of the earth
between your shoulders, my Atlas.
Your stumbles come more frequently now,
often enough that I fear we may never
rise again. May never walk step-by-step again.

Your hands, etched like the stories of peaks and valleys
on those contour maps we pour over to wonder
what it would have been like to wander there,
are cracked and calloused, and I see the blood
briefly before you tuck your hand behind you
and wipe it on your pant leg. The veins
on the back distend and rise up, working.

Your eyes look down more than up these days,
searching for something you may have dropped
or something you thought you once had
only to have lost. The edges have their own

ridges and gullies, and red rivers meander
to-and-fro in the white. They see the next
step, but maybe not the one after, or after that.

I heard you groan when you awoke this morning,
and your joints popped and cracked and creaked
until you shut the bathroom door to let me sleep.
Before you turned on the fan, I heard you sigh,
a long release I imagined where everything
was perfect, no toils, no troubles, no aches,
no schedules, no burdens to carry, no weight.

A Task I Did Not Want

It was a task I did not want
waiting on the platform after the rain
came earlier. The afternoon clung to my skin,
muggy and heavy and acrid like the afternoons
on that small island in the Philippines
I never can remember the name to.

But the evening started with a breeze
still thick but much cooler in the gray
after twilight and just before the night
has settled its dark curtain over the landscape.
A few stars and the dim yellow lights echo
back, not like diamonds. More like clouded
and yellowed cubic zirconia you can find
in costume jewelry. And it's quiet now.

No rushing to-and-fro into the city or even
fleeing its bright lights and synthetic noises,
beating like an industrialized and mechanical heart
you push into the background. The last train came,

rumbling and creaking and squealing to a stop.
I waited around the corner because I didn't want
to speak with anyone on the empty platform.
I watched into the side window and out the front
as the porter stepped down off the train,
and without so much as a pause to call out

he set down that beige valise I bought for you
on my trip to Milan. For a moment I thought
he looked familiar, then I remembered how often
I travel this same line day in and day out.
The train left without any other soul getting on
or getting off, and I walked out to stand alone,
wondering why you hadn't come and why
I left without looking in what was left behind.

Broken and Scattered and Strewn

I've tried to hide from the storm
hands trembling like the rumbling of the thunder
my fingers cupped over my ears
do not keep out the sirens.
My bones are brittle, and I taste blood
where I must have bit my lip
when all those things were broken and shattered and strewn
about across the floor where neglect forgot them.

Dystopian Strawberries

I watched you pick the gravel from the strawberry rash
on your knee but I didn't see you fall or stumble
while the rain fell in sheets or buckets or tropical torrents
that hid any sharpness to your shape behind a gray curtain
that swallowed you up into a blur of obscurity.
I thought I heard you whimper, but it could have been the storms
or something deep and guttural that started in the bottom
of your chest and rumbled up through your heart
and tumbled from your lips and rode between the thunder.
They have always said these are the moments that define us:
what we do for others when no one watches
what we do when we are not judged or expected.
This dystopian world rages around us, and I only watch
and wonder if I influence to the good or to the ill.

To and Fro

They hung a man yesterday who said he'd die free
while he spat at all of us who still lived
while he still hung, to and fro in the wind
that gusted up through the square, carrying with it
a grit that caught in my hair and I felt it
upon my lips—they cracked when I grimaced
the moment the trapdoor opened and the rope snapped
his body to a sudden stop at the end of the fall.
My father once told me he wasn't afraid of falling;
it was the landing that made him shiver with fright.
Where is his freedom now? I wonder aloud and know
that his last taste was of freedom. He is free from sight:
he will no longer see his family suffer from hunger;
he will no longer see his family shiver in the winter.
His ears deaf to the symphony of sounds he once heard:
never again will he hear his infant cry because her mother
has gone dry; never again will he hear the weeping of his wife
because she cannot suck her babe at her flaccid breasts.
He is free now. His period of indentured service has ended.
I turn and walk away from the swinging man—to-and-fro—
not realizing I am patting the silver in my pocket until later.

Traveling Diet of Instances

The connection between food and memory astonishes
even me. Places I have been.
Even more places I have grown.

I remember Griesheim, Germany through sliced onions
dipped in mustard, sharing them
with my sister as we hid from mother
because we just knew we were living
on the edge, and spaghetti in a white sauce,
and the aroma of cooking sausages
as I walked through the fair at Nuremberg,
and the Geburtstagskuchen for my twelfth birthday.
But most vividly, and with complete clarity,
the *Coca-cola* while I waited in the white plastic
chair at the airport terminal.

Iceland is just a memory.
My parents sent me to learn to ride
like a gentleman—I know this because we ate
rhubarb soup with every evening meal.

The land of fire and ice—
and tasting baby oysters for the first time,
and last, eating them one at a time,
speared on toothpicks, three whole tins
until we became sick from the goodness.
It was fish every friday
and plates of steaming potato fries
in Reykjavik by the city lake
where the ducks swam even in winter,
their furiously, frantically paddling feet
keeping just one tiny corner free from freezing.

Memory of my first family passing
is tied up with the way angel food cake
seems to melt easily when it is warm.
It is the ribeye steak the very last time
I saw my friend in Kansas City,
dinner downtown at the Cigar Box
where retired men ate and drank
and listened to the retired lounge singer sing
Mack the Knife and Frank Sinatra covers.

Memory is a book of recipes—
in no certain order
but worn, familiar pages.

A Beautiful Life

I cannot remember all the things I have tried to be—
all the little things wrapped up inside my mind my heart my soul
like little treasures, treasures waiting to be unlocked,
only I cannot find the key—for her for them for every one but me,
for all the imagined goals and dreams and destinations
of every single satisfaction-guaranteed-demanding existence.

The rain is black again, here behind enemy lines,
where the world has grayed out
and memory has all but faded.
Loneliness has become my roommate, my teddy bear
—a dance with the reflection with an eye full of emptiness—
and waiting brings no forgiveness
in this forest of skeletal-faced trees
that reach out to me just for a single, empty embrace
—only solitude and vacancy.

And today tastes like the ashes of bones in my mouth
parched and thirsting for the water of life,
brought to me—this poor, wasted, pathetic wretch—

98

in a clay jug by some Sicilian beauty

as I sit beside this dusty road because my shoes

have worn through and my feet have started to bleed.

Playing Chess in Bryant Park

When I go to New York I notice these little pockets:
Places amidst the hustle and the bustle and the chaos
where time slows to something much more manageable
than the frenzied day-to-day flashes blurring in motion,
two worlds, all the same but as different from each other
as the two sides of the same quarter flipped to decide fate.

Bryant Park in the fall before the heat of summer fades:
Two players stepped out of the rush and settled down
into white plastic chairs played without a clock to conquer
one over the other. The jet stream of flesh and machinery
powered past endlessly and without pause, without slowing,
except for their careful moves and guarded steps and challenges
or the people that pulled themselves from the flow to watch
two strangers battle and work magic and slow the perpetual surge.

Ferrara's on the cusp of two worlds late in the dark of night:
Italian ice and gelato and pastries and chocolate-covered cannoli,
a place as old as dirt but bright enough to hold back the night.
Little hidden alcoves and paths in the expansive Central Park:

Gapstow Bridge over the Pond when the stones are frosted with ice
and the water edges sparkle in the sun. Inscope Arch
in the early morning hours as the sun peaks in and out, dancing
through the leaves of trees and hedges creeping in from the sides.
The cobblestoned entrance to the zoo before its Saturday opening
with its brick guard shack and lined with green benches.
Bethesda Terrace in those quiet moments it is only you
walking the echoing walk from stairs to arches to fountain.

And a certain upstairs corridor in an old New York building
where my hands trembled because I feared to knock
or enter unannounced because I wanted to be good enough.

Listening to Voices

I thought I heard your voice between the gaps in the thunder
something that edged on pain, something resembling a long moan
  of loss
like those times a person hears his own name in a crowded place
filled elbow to elbow with people milling and talking and laughing
and he turns to see who called out, only they all look elsewhere,
they all turn and walk away, and not a one has called out to him.

Sometimes I hear a melody or a tune, but I cannot sing
the words that I only mumble and I move my lips as if I knew them
and any casual observer either thinks I do or thinks me mad,
like that man on the subway platform that speaks to you as you
  pass,
only he has sidestepped because his side of the conversation is
  three responses
into a future you haven't yet lived, a seer or a fortune teller
no one listens to and the listeners simply smile and move to the
  other side.

102

I thought I heard your voice the other day when the rain stopped,

and I wondered if you said something cryptic or maybe even
  prophetic

but in the end it may have been as uncomplicated as asking
  whether or not

I had turned off the iron and closed the drapes before I left.

Travel Lodge in Chicago

Marshmallows belong in hot chocolate
I learned one cold January day in the ashes of the Blizzard of '79
because of course it was the perfect time for the transmission to
   fail;

And that nice woman in her glaring orange dress
with a black apron with deep and wide pockets
and thick rubber-soled shoes that remind me more of hospitals
than motel restaurants asked me if I wanted them in my cocoa.

When I looked to you for guidance
as a ten-year-old boy often does before he grows too wise
only four or five years later, you shrugged and said: Try them.
Decades later I know it wasn't an indifferent shrug of an uncaring
   father,
but one that told me that there would always be unknowns,
adventures that we would take together.

Marshmallows do belong in hot chocolate,
especially on days where over twenty inches of snow crunch

beneath a young boy's feet with every step

and the wind off the lake on a bright, crisp day

blows just hard enough to grasp your breath away.

How Long I Suffered to Rid the Pain

Time changes the concept of itself as we collect more.
My first watch was something grand, something I cherished
because I held on my wrist the power to understand
what the thing all the big people felt slipping away meant.
We say it slips away as if it were tangible and could be grasped
within the clutches of our grasping and clutching and kneading
  fingers,
slipping away as if we can keep it from escaping or being free.

But our hold is tenuous at its strongest
because what we have is brittle and crumbles in our hands.
More and more of this conceptual we latch onto
—we read books to learn how to do more with less,
we change our methods and schedules to recapture some—
only to have it fall away to the side squandered and wasted
where we wished we knew its importance while we still held
  plenty,
before we started chasing it.

106

My first watch told time with its click, click, clicking second hand
and the gradually-moving minute hand I once had the patience
to watch shift from one number to the next
and the hour hand that moves only after I look away.
Time—the more you chase it, the faster it flees into the shadows
and the further away it stays. And if we wait long enough
even the tears dry, leaving a trail of salt upon our cheeks.

Notes on Eating

Hunched over with her elbows pulled in,
holding the food in both hands in front of her
and taking tiny bits while following
the conversation with her darting eyes.

Each time she turned to the man beside her
she pulled her head back like being that close
to him filled too much of her vision. She looked
across the table and her neck came back forward,
and the muscles relaxed from the tight cords.

He didn't realize a piece of bread clung tightly
to his seven-o'clock whiskers and no one said
anything to him but they all watched the crumb
like they found it disturbing or even disgusting.
When he spoke, it jumped up and down precariously
but hung with all its organic seven-grain might,
refusing to tumble off into the oblivion of refuse.
No one listens to his story or hears his words
and he still feels they want to know more and more

so he continues, his smile growing and beaming

from all the attention he hasn't deserved or earned.

When it does plunge to the table, she blinks and blinks,

watching it fall. With her attention removed, he smiles

and lifts the napkin to dab at the corner of his mouth

never understanding or realizing it is all too late.

Couch Magic

They say all kinds of magic things can be found
waiting beneath the cushions of the tattered couch
sitting in the middle of your grandmother's living room—
not just lint and string and the crumbs from Papa's
toasted bacon and peanut butter and banana sandwich
she told him not once but one thousand times to eat
at the kitchen table where it was meant to be eaten,
but sometimes treasure, as much as a dollar thirty-seven
in five silvery quarters from North Dakota, Delaware
and three from all the way up in Alaska, a dime
and two shiny pennies that hadn't lost their luster.

I once though to myself: If treasure hides among the cushions,
what might be behind the frilly skirt on the bottom edge?
So this is where Sadie puts all her chewed up tennis balls,
under the couch amongst your brother's diecast '68 Mustang
and the USB power converter I can't seem to figure out
and the missing left shoe from your cousin's little doll.

But hiding back behind that middle leg that seems so useless
is a tiny action figure, one of those movie knock-offs
—not the real deal, just different enough to avoid litigation—
and I remember that time you also looked behind the skirt,
calmly saying: Hi, Guy. There you are. I cannot recall
ever seeing your grandmother's eyes getting so big
when she feared magic things may live beneath her couch.

The Gurney

She wept the first time it happened. Curled up in a ball
beside the gurney staring at the reaching hand above her
where it had fallen from beneath the white linen sheet.
The creaking could have been the front wheel on the right,
the one that needed oil or grease because it spun
and shook when the other three worked as they should.

It could have been old bones scraping against joints
or tendons that had lost lubrication like the wheel.
No one ever told her the gurney had a forward or backward,
or even a left or a right. She never wondered why
she pushed from the back. That's just the way it should be.
Truth was there was no front or back. She determined
long ago the front became the front because just as in life

the head looked to the fore. She felt they needed to see
where it was they were going, into glory or into an abyss
—they should not see what they left behind, it could hold them
here and could not be rewritten or redone or renewed.
But some reached out still trying to hold on to something

left unfinished or unsaid or unrealized. She knew they had stories,
but no one ever came to her with them so she could speak

words over them so they wouldn't be alone. They needed words,
they needed to know someone would remember them
remember that they had been here, that they had lived
that they had loved that they had wept that they had smiled.
When no one comes to get them and she is the last voice
to be spoken over them, she tells their stories for them.

This is Mrs. Bonaventure who once saw the sun rise
and drive out the shadows that clung to the stones of Machu
  Picchu,
and she rode a burro down the narrow trails along the walls
of the Grand Canyon and swam in the turquoise waters
of Havasu Falls with the love of her life, and she stood
six hours in the rain when they buried him at Arlington.
This is Mr. Marciano who lived his life alone but at night

listened to the stars in the sky above, watching as the Aurora
danced and weaved and twisted and changed hues and streaks
from blue to green to orange to red. He wrote music
and played for no one but himself because it brought him joy.
He looked up because to look down was to be mired
in the muck and grime of the remains left behind.

When her day comes—when the world is quiet and dreaming

like it is now—she wonders who will speak her words,

who will tell her story, who will remember. What of the day

she lies here and no one comes to claim her?

Will she try to cry out from beneath the sheet: No!

This is wrong! This is wrong! This is wrong?

Will she live to be gray and wrinkled with loose muscles

Of bundled tissue? Will her skin grow flaccid and slack

at the end? Or will she be beautiful? Will she be struck down

too early and in her prime? Too young or too old?

Now when it happens she holds the hand, telling them

all will be okay and not to hold too tight, because this world,

this place, is lonely and fragile and weak. Look forward not back.

She says to them: I will take you to the edge but you must go first

  so

you can show me the way when I take these same steps for the

  very last time.

The list of people who have influenced my poetry is immense—all those living and those that have lived even before I came screaming into this world and those that have now passed into the beyond. From reading Chaucer in Middle English to writing a paper on Williams Wordsworth's *A Slumber Did My Spirit Seal* where I argued with my professor Skip Hayes that it wasn't about death but about life to Ai Ogawa and Billy Collins. From the elderly gentleman shuffling through the bookstore quietly mumbling while he read from a magazine to the man that wore a heavy coat no matter the weather while he walked his dog. All these and more have contributed to the ideas that mull about in my mind until I get them out on paper. For them, I am very grateful.

I would also like to thank the members of the critique group Authors Anonymous 2.0 for listening to my works and offering suggestions or support. I would like to thank Venessa Cerasale for her help in getting this mess all compiled in a readable format. And most of all, I want to thank my family for their support. My wife and soulmate Chrissi for her patience and tolerance of my absentmindedness. My children Hayley and Edan for their love and support. My granddaughter Rabbit for being the embodiment of love and joy.

JC Crumpton is the award-winning author of the novels *Silence in the Garden* and the upcoming *Slipping the Cradle* and collection *Cardboard Heroes*. Born in southern California, he grew up all over the world and currently resides in Northwest Arkansas with his wife. JC earned a degree in English with a Creative Writing Emphasis from the University of Arkansas.